Mayor Eric Adams

His Life Story, Charges, and the Bribery Scandal that Shattered New York's Political Future

---

Roger J. Soliz

TABLE OF CONTENT

Introduction

Setting the Stage: The Rise and Fall of Eric Adams

The political career of Eric Adams, once seen as a promising leader and a symbol of change for New York City, has taken a dramatic and unexpected turn. His rise to power was swift and inspiring, filled with promises of a new era of leadership, but his fall from grace has been equally rapid and shocking. From his humble beginnings in Brooklyn to the halls of Gracie Mansion, Adams's story is one of ambition, perseverance, and, ultimately, controversy.

Eric Adams was born into a working-class family in Brooklyn, a borough that would later become the heart of his political career. Raised by a single mother who worked multiple jobs to support her family, Adams's early life was shaped by the struggles of the working poor in a city rife with inequality. He faced challenges that many young Black men in New York City experienced, including encounters with the police that would later influence his career in law enforcement and politics.

As a young man, Adams joined the New York City Police Department (NYPD), where he quickly rose through the ranks. His time as a police officer was marked by his advocacy for reform within the force. He was outspoken about the need for changes in how the police treated minority communities, often clashing with his superiors and drawing attention to issues of racial injustice long before they became mainstream political topics. Adams co-founded 100 Blacks in Law Enforcement Who Care, an organization aimed at addressing racial profiling and advocating for fairness in law enforcement practices. This experience would later define his mayoral campaign, as he positioned himself as both tough on crime and a reformer with a deep understanding of the city's policing issues.

After his time in the NYPD, Adams transitioned into politics. His journey was not without its challenges, but his determination and ability to connect with New Yorkers from all walks of life helped him build a loyal following. He was elected Brooklyn Borough President in 2013, a role that allowed him to further develop his political platform and expand his influence. During his tenure, Adams became known for his progressive views on housing, public health, and criminal justice reform, often aligning himself with the broader national movement toward equity and social justice. He spoke openly about his personal health journey, promoting plant-based diets and wellness as tools for combating chronic illness, and he used his platform to advocate for policies that would improve the health and well-being of all New Yorkers.

In 2021, Adams ran for mayor of New York City, positioning himself as the candidate who could bring balance to a city divided by crime, inequality, and the lingering effects of the COVID-19 pandemic. His message resonated with voters who were tired of political gridlock and rising crime rates. Adams presented himself as a bridge between the progressive wing of the Democratic Party and those who wanted more traditional approaches to law and order. He won the mayoral election, becoming the second Black mayor in the city's history and promising to lead New York into a new era of safety, prosperity, and inclusivity.

However, his time in office was marked by challenges from the start. New York City was grappling with multiple crises, including an increase in violent crime, ongoing economic recovery from the pandemic, and growing tensions around issues like homelessness and immigration. Adams's administration sought to tackle these issues head-on, with mixed results. His tough-on-crime stance, which had initially helped him win the mayoral seat, began to alienate some of his more progressive supporters. At the same time, his reformist agenda did not sit well with more conservative factions. The mayor found himself walking a political tightrope, trying to satisfy both sides of the city's deeply divided political spectrum.

As Adams tried to navigate these political challenges, reports began to surface about potential improprieties in his campaign fundraising. What began as whispers of questionable donations soon escalated into a full-blown federal investigation. The public was shocked when, in 2024, Adams was indicted on multiple charges, including wire fraud, bribery, and accepting illegal campaign contributions from foreign sources. The indictment sent shockwaves through New York's political landscape and raised serious questions about the integrity of the mayor and his administration.

For many, the news of the indictment was a stunning fall from grace for a man who had once been seen as a beacon of hope for New York City. His supporters, particularly those in Brooklyn who had followed his career closely, were left grappling with the reality that the leader they had believed in was now facing serious criminal charges. Adams maintained his innocence, asserting that the charges were politically motivated and that he had always followed the law. Yet, the damage to his reputation was undeniable, and the scandal quickly became the defining narrative of his mayoral tenure.

The charges against Adams not only threatened his career but also cast a shadow over the future of New York City politics. As the mayor fought to clear his name, his ability to govern effectively was called into question. The city, already facing significant challenges, was now saddled with a leader whose attention was divided between running the city and defending himself in court. Political opponents seized on the scandal, using it as ammunition in their efforts to unseat him and to challenge the broader Democratic leadership in the state.

The rise and fall of Eric Adams is a cautionary tale of the complexities of political life in one of the world's most demanding cities. His journey from a Brooklyn street kid to the highest office in New York City is a testament to his resilience and ambition. Yet, his downfall, marked by allegations of corruption and betrayal of the public trust, serves as a stark reminder of the fragility of political power. As Adams faces the legal battles ahead, the city watches, wondering what the future holds for its once-promising mayor and for the political landscape of New York itself.

From Brooklyn to the NYPD: Adams's Path to Public Service

Eric Adams's journey from a working-class upbringing in Brooklyn to his eventual rise as a public figure in New York City is a story of determination, grit, and unwavering commitment to public service. Born in 1960 in Brownsville, Brooklyn, Adams's early years were shaped by the environment in which he grew up—an area known for its challenges with poverty, crime, and a strained relationship between its residents and law enforcement. These formative experiences played a critical role in shaping his worldview and desire to make a difference, especially within the realms of justice and community relations.

Growing up, Adams was no stranger to hardship. He lived in a small, crowded apartment with his five siblings and single mother, Dorothy Adams, who worked long hours as a house cleaner to make ends meet. As a young boy, Adams quickly became familiar with the difficulties faced by many families like his—struggles to pay rent, access to quality education, and the ever-present tension between residents and police. Brownsville in the 1960s was not an easy place to live, especially for a young Black boy. Crime rates were high, and the relationship between law enforcement and the community was often strained. For many young men like Adams, the future seemed uncertain, but his mother instilled in him a strong sense of purpose and a desire to rise above the circumstances of his environment.

One of the pivotal moments in Adams's youth came when he was just 15 years old. He and his older brother, Conrad, were arrested for trespassing. What should have been a minor infraction turned into a traumatic experience when both boys were taken to a police station and severely beaten by officers. This experience left a lasting impression on Adams, igniting a deep sense of anger but also a desire to change the system from within. Rather than succumbing to the bitterness of that moment, Adams would later recount how the incident became a turning point that motivated him to pursue a career in law enforcement. He felt that, to bring about real change, he needed to be on the inside, helping to reform the very institution that had wronged him.

Despite the challenges of his early life, Adams remained focused on his education. He attended Bayside High School in Queens, where he began to channel his experiences into a desire for activism and community involvement. After graduating, he went on to study at New York City Technical College and later John Jay College of Criminal Justice, where he obtained degrees in criminal justice. His time at John Jay solidified his commitment to addressing the systemic issues that plagued the criminal justice system, particularly its treatment of minorities.

In 1984, Adams took the first significant step toward his goal of reforming law enforcement by joining the New York City Police Department (NYPD). His decision to enter the force was met with skepticism by some in his community. At a time when the NYPD was seen as an adversarial presence in many minority neighborhoods, Adams's choice to wear the badge seemed counterintuitive to some. However, for Adams, becoming a police officer was a strategic decision—he believed that meaningful change could only come from within. He entered the force determined to challenge the status quo and improve the relationship between police officers and the communities they served.

Adams's early years with the NYPD were not without struggle. As a young Black officer, he faced the internal racism and biases that were common within the department at the time. But instead of backing down, Adams pushed forward, working to rise through the ranks while maintaining his commitment to reform. Over his 22-year career with the NYPD, he gained a reputation for his outspoken criticism of the department's treatment of minority communities. In the early 1990s, Adams co-founded 100 Blacks in Law Enforcement Who Care, an advocacy group within the NYPD that focused on addressing issues of police brutality, racial profiling, and the need for reform within the department.

Through this platform, Adams became an outspoken voice for police accountability. He frequently called for more diversity within the department and better training for officers to deal with the complexities of policing in racially diverse neighborhoods. His activism often put him at odds with the police leadership, but he remained undeterred. Adams was not afraid to challenge the institution from within, even when it meant risking his career. His leadership within 100 Blacks in Law Enforcement Who Care earned him respect both within and outside the department, particularly in communities of color, where many saw him as a rare advocate who truly understood their struggles with law enforcement.

As his career with the NYPD progressed, Adams continued to build a reputation as both a reformer and a bridge-builder. He understood the unique challenges that police officers faced, but he also knew the pain and distrust that many in the community felt toward law enforcement. This dual perspective allowed him to advocate for reforms that sought to bring about meaningful change without alienating the officers tasked with carrying out their duties. Adams was a strong proponent of community policing, believing that officers needed to form positive relationships with the communities they served to effectively reduce crime and rebuild trust.

Adams retired from the NYPD in 2006 with the rank of captain, but his career in public service was far from over. His experiences on the force had deepened his desire to enact broader systemic change, and he turned his attention to politics as a way to continue his advocacy for reform. In 2007, he was elected to the New York State Senate, representing the 20th District in Brooklyn. His time in the Senate allowed him to continue his work on criminal justice reform, while also expanding his focus to other issues impacting his constituents, such as affordable housing, education, and healthcare.

During his four terms in the Senate, Adams championed legislation aimed at improving police accountability, increasing access to healthcare for underserved communities, and expanding economic opportunities for marginalized populations. His time in Albany further established him as a rising star in New York politics, and in 2013, he made history by becoming the first Black person to be elected Brooklyn Borough President.

As Borough President, Adams continued to advocate for criminal justice reform, but he also expanded his focus to include public health, affordable housing, and economic development. He launched several initiatives aimed at improving the quality of life for Brooklyn residents, including efforts to reduce gun violence, improve access to healthy food, and support small businesses. Adams used his platform to address the disparities that existed in Brooklyn, particularly between the wealthier and more impoverished neighborhoods, and worked tirelessly to create more equitable opportunities for all residents.

Throughout his career, Eric Adams's journey from Brooklyn to the NYPD, and eventually into politics, has been defined by his commitment to public service and reform. His early life experiences, particularly his encounter with police brutality, fueled his desire to change the system from within. As both a police officer and a politician, Adams has consistently fought for the rights of marginalized communities and sought to build bridges between law enforcement and the public. His path to public service has not been an easy one, but his resilience and dedication to justice have made him a key figure in New York City's political landscape.

As his story unfolds, the complexities of his life and career provide insight into how a man with a deep commitment to reform can rise to power, while also facing the challenges that come with being a public servant in a city as dynamic and demanding as New York. Adams's journey is a testament to the power of perseverance and the importance of fighting for justice, even when the odds seem insurmountable.

Chapter 2: The Political Ascent

The Journey from Borough President to Mayor of New York City

Eric Adams's rise in New York City politics is a story of persistence, vision, and determination. His journey from serving as the Brooklyn Borough President to becoming the Mayor of the largest city in the United States reflects his ambition and the deep connection he developed with the communities he aimed to serve. His path to the mayoralty was not linear, nor was it without its challenges, but Adams's ability to navigate the turbulent waters of New York City politics ultimately led him to the position of one of the most powerful political figures in the country.

Before his time as Brooklyn Borough President, Adams had already established himself as a key figure in law enforcement. A former NYPD captain, Adams's time in the police force provided him with critical insight into the systemic issues plaguing New York City, particularly in the areas of public safety, racial justice, and community policing. This experience also allowed him to connect with various demographics across the city, from the wealthy enclaves of Brooklyn Heights to the working-class neighbourhoods of East New York. His ability to communicate with and understand the concerns of everyday New Yorkers played a central role in his early political career.

When Adams took office as Brooklyn Borough President in 2014, he inherited a borough undergoing significant changes. Brooklyn, long seen as a symbol of working-class New York, had transformed into a hub of gentrification and rapid development. This transformation brought new challenges, including increased housing prices, rising inequality, and tensions between long-time residents and the influx of new, wealthier residents. Adams positioned himself as a bridge between these two worlds, advocating for policies that would protect vulnerable communities while promoting economic growth.

During his tenure as Brooklyn Borough President, Adams focused on a variety of issues that resonated with the borough's residents. Affordable housing, economic development, and public health were among his key priorities. He championed the expansion of affordable housing projects, recognising that rising rent prices were pushing out long-time residents and disproportionately affecting communities of colour. Adams worked to balance the competing interests of developers and residents, often walking a tightrope between encouraging investment in Brooklyn's future while safeguarding its diverse, working-class roots.

Adams also became known for his passionate advocacy for healthier lifestyles, a cause close to his heart after he was diagnosed with type 2 diabetes in 2016. Rather than succumb to the disease, Adams overhauled his diet and reversed many of his symptoms, becoming a vocal proponent of plant-based diets. He leveraged his personal experience to promote health initiatives across Brooklyn, encouraging residents to adopt healthier habits, and even pushing for changes in the city's public institutions, such as schools and hospitals, to offer more nutritious food options.

His leadership as borough president was marked by his ability to connect with people on a personal level. He wasn't a distant politician; he was often seen walking the streets, engaging with residents, and attending community events. Adams understood the importance of visibility and accessibility in politics. His frequent appearances in local neighbourhoods, along with his active social media presence, allowed him to build a base of loyal supporters who viewed him not just as a politician but as a public servant deeply committed to the wellbeing of Brooklyn.

As his profile grew, so too did his ambition. It became clear that Adams had his eyes on the mayoralty, and he began laying the groundwork for a citywide campaign. His time as Brooklyn Borough President had given him a platform to showcase his leadership and vision for New York City. In particular, his focus on public safety resonated with many voters, especially in the wake of rising crime rates and the growing debate over police reform. Adams's unique position as a former police officer turned reform advocate allowed him to appeal to both sides of the law enforcement debate – those calling for increased safety measures and those demanding accountability and change within the NYPD.

The 2021 mayoral race was a crowded field, with numerous high-profile candidates vying for the Democratic nomination. Adams's campaign stood out for its focus on law and order, as well as his personal story of overcoming adversity. He leaned into his narrative as a self-made man from humble beginnings, who had risen through the ranks of the NYPD and eventually into political office. This resonated with many working-class New Yorkers, particularly in the outer boroughs, who felt left behind by the city's political elite.

Adams's message of safety and stability came at a crucial moment for New York City. In the wake of the COVID-19 pandemic, the city was grappling with a host of challenges – economic uncertainty, rising crime rates, and growing social unrest. Adams positioned himself as the candidate best suited to lead the city through this difficult time. He promised to restore order, support the police while pushing for necessary reforms, and rebuild the city's economy. His platform appealed to voters across a wide spectrum, from progressives concerned with social justice to moderates seeking stability and growth.

Throughout the campaign, Adams's experience as a former police officer became both a strength and a point of contention. While some saw it as a qualification that uniquely positioned him to address the city's crime issues, others viewed it as a sign that he might be too aligned with law enforcement to push for the reforms needed to address police brutality and systemic racism. Adams walked a fine line, advocating for reforms within the police department while also making clear his support for officers who were doing their jobs ethically and responsibly. His nuanced position on this issue allowed him to capture votes from a wide range of New Yorkers, particularly those who were concerned about both crime and police misconduct.

Adams's victory in the Democratic primary all but secured his path to the mayoralty, given the city's overwhelming Democratic voter base. However, his win was not without its controversies. Questions about his residency, finances, and campaign donations dogged him throughout the race. Despite these challenges, Adams maintained his focus on the issues that mattered most to voters – crime, housing, and economic recovery. He ran a disciplined campaign that kept him in the spotlight and positioned him as the frontrunner for most of the race.

On January 1, 2022, Eric Adams was sworn in as the 110th mayor of New York City. His inauguration marked a new chapter in the city's history, as he became only the second African-American mayor to hold the position. Adams's victory was seen by many as a triumph of perseverance and resilience – the culmination of a long and often difficult political journey. He had successfully navigated the complexities of New York City politics, building a broad coalition of supporters and positioning himself as a leader capable of steering the city through challenging times.

However, as with any political ascent, Adams's victory came with high expectations and significant challenges. New York City was still reeling from the effects of the pandemic, and the issues of crime, inequality, and public health that had dominated his campaign remained at the forefront of the city's concerns. Adams faced the daunting task of not only delivering on his promises but also proving that he could lead the city through one of its most difficult periods in recent memory.

Eric Adams's journey from Brooklyn Borough President to Mayor of New York City is a testament to his determination and his ability to connect with the people of New York. His ascent to the mayoralty was not without its obstacles, but Adams's focus on public safety, health, and economic recovery resonated with a city in need of strong leadership. His time as mayor would ultimately be shaped by the very issues that had defined his campaign – and the public's expectations for how he would address them.

Chapter 3: Eric Adams's Vision for New York

Campaign Promises, Policies, and the Push for Change

When Eric Adams launched his campaign for mayor of New York City, he positioned himself as a bridge between two distinct visions for the city. On one hand, there was the need for continued reform, particularly in the face of economic disparity, policing, and racial injustice. On the other, there was a desire to preserve public safety and ensure that the city continued to recover from the devastating effects of the COVID-19 pandemic. Adams, with his background as a former police officer and his tenure as Brooklyn Borough President, seemed uniquely qualified to navigate these sometimes conflicting priorities. He pledged to be a mayor who could address both sides of the equation, appealing to progressives who wanted change and moderates who sought stability.

Adams's vision for New York City was deeply rooted in his own life experiences. As someone who grew up in poverty, faced police brutality, and rose through the ranks to become a leading public figure, his personal story shaped his policy positions. His platform was built on tackling the city's most pressing challenges: crime, inequality, public health, and economic recovery. He frequently highlighted his journey from hardship to leadership as a way of connecting with everyday New Yorkers who felt disconnected from the political elite. His campaign was driven by a desire to create a New York that worked for all its residents, not just those at the top.

One of Adams's major campaign promises was his focus on public safety. As a former police officer, he understood both the importance of law enforcement and the need for reform. He walked a delicate line, advocating for a strong police presence to combat rising crime rates, while also acknowledging the need to address systemic issues within the police force. His stance on policing was one of the defining features of his campaign. Adams positioned himself as someone who could bring real change from within, as he had firsthand experience of both the problems and the potential solutions. He believed that police reform was possible without sacrificing public safety and that the two could coexist to create a safer, fairer city.

Adams's approach to policing was rooted in his belief that community engagement and law enforcement needed to work hand-in-hand. He often spoke about his vision of "precision policing," a strategy that focused on targeting the individuals and areas most responsible for crime, rather than implementing broad, heavy-handed policing tactics. He was a proponent of investing in technology and intelligence-based policing to make the city safer without resorting to tactics that alienated communities, particularly communities of colour. At the same time, Adams argued for increased accountability within the police force, ensuring that officers who abused their power would face consequences.

Beyond policing, Adams's vision for New York extended to economic recovery. The city was reeling from the impact of the COVID-19 pandemic, which had left businesses struggling, unemployment rates high, and many New Yorkers uncertain about their future. Adams made it clear that reviving the city's economy was a top priority. He was particularly focused on creating opportunities for the working class and those who had been hit hardest by the pandemic. His economic plan revolved around investing in job creation, supporting small businesses, and ensuring that New York remained an attractive place for corporations and entrepreneurs alike.

Adams saw small businesses as the backbone of the city's economy, and he pledged to make it easier for them to thrive. His campaign promised to cut through the bureaucratic red tape that often made it difficult for small business owners to succeed in New York. He proposed reducing fines and fees, simplifying the licensing process, and providing more support to entrepreneurs. Adams also emphasised the importance of creating pathways to success for workers in industries like hospitality, retail, and transportation, which had been particularly devastated by the pandemic. His goal was to create a New York where economic opportunities were accessible to all, regardless of background or zip code.

In addition to economic recovery, Adams's platform included a strong emphasis on public health. The COVID-19 pandemic had exposed glaring inequalities in the city's healthcare system, with low-income communities and communities of colour bearing the brunt of the virus's impact. Adams's experience growing up in a community with limited access to healthcare informed his commitment to addressing these disparities. He pledged to improve access to healthcare across the city, particularly in underserved areas, and to ensure that the lessons learned from the pandemic would lead to a stronger, more equitable healthcare system moving forward.

Adams also recognised the importance of addressing the city's mental health crisis. He spoke openly about the need for a more comprehensive approach to mental health services, particularly for the city's homeless population. During his campaign, Adams pledged to expand mental health services and integrate them more effectively with other social services. His vision for New York included not just a focus on physical health but also on the mental well-being of its residents, recognising that mental health care is a critical component of a thriving city.

Education was another cornerstone of Adams's vision for New York. He understood that the key to long-term success for the city lay in its schools. Adams frequently spoke about the need to invest in education, particularly for students from low-income backgrounds. He advocated for expanding early childhood education, increasing funding for schools in disadvantaged areas, and improving access to vocational training programs. His goal was to create an education system that prepared all students, regardless of their socioeconomic status, for success in the modern economy. Adams was particularly passionate about the need to close the achievement gap and ensure that all students had the resources and support they needed to thrive.

Housing affordability was another major issue Adams sought to tackle. New York City's housing crisis had been worsening for years, with skyrocketing rents and limited affordable housing options pushing many residents out of their communities. Adams's vision for New York included a comprehensive plan to increase affordable housing options and ensure that New Yorkers could continue to live in the city without being priced out. He proposed policies that would incentivise developers to build more affordable housing, particularly in areas that had been gentrified. Adams also emphasised the importance of protecting tenants' rights and ensuring that the city's rent control laws were enforced fairly.

Throughout his campaign, Adams maintained that his vision for New York was one of inclusivity. He wanted to create a city where everyone, regardless of their background, had the opportunity to succeed. His personal story as someone who had risen from poverty to a position of leadership was a central part of his appeal. He framed his policies as part of a larger effort to create a more equitable city, where the needs of the working class and the most vulnerable were prioritised. Adams's vision for New York was one where the city's wealth and resources were distributed more fairly, and where every New Yorker had a stake in the city's future.

However, Adams's vision was not without its critics. Some felt that his policies on policing did not go far enough in addressing systemic issues, while others worried that his focus on public safety might come at the expense of civil liberties. Similarly, his economic plans, while ambitious, were seen by some as unrealistic, particularly given the city's ongoing budget challenges. Nevertheless, Adams remained steadfast in his belief that he was the right leader to guide New York through its recovery and into a more prosperous future.

In the end, Adams's campaign was about more than just policy proposals. It was about his vision of a city that could overcome its challenges and emerge stronger, more inclusive, and more resilient. His promises of reform, safety, and economic recovery resonated with many voters, particularly those who felt that the city had been left behind in the wake of the pandemic. As he took office, Adams carried with him the hopes of millions of New Yorkers who believed in his vision for a better, safer, and more just city. However, as his tenure as mayor progressed, it became clear that fulfilling these promises would be a complex and difficult task.

Chapter 4: The Investigation Begins
Federal Scrutiny

How the Bribery Allegations Surfaced

The rise of Eric Adams to the highest office in New York City was not just an individual success story; it represented a moment of optimism for many New Yorkers who believed in his message of safety, economic revival, and equity. Adams, a former police officer who had become Brooklyn's borough president before winning the mayoralty, seemed to embody the potential of a public servant who understood the complexities of law enforcement while still advocating for progressive policies. However, behind the scenes, federal investigators were piecing together a troubling narrative—one that would ultimately shake the very foundations of New York's political system.

The investigation into Adams didn't begin overnight. In fact, it was the result of years of quiet scrutiny. The seeds of suspicion were planted during his time as Brooklyn borough president, a position he held from 2014 to 2021. While Adams was building a reputation as a reformer and advocate for social justice, investigators were slowly picking up on irregularities in his campaign finances. At first, these issues were minor—small donations from questionable sources or the occasional missed paperwork. But over time, a pattern began to emerge, one that federal agents couldn't ignore.

It wasn't just the campaign donations that caught the attention of investigators. Adams had always been a larger-than-life figure, and his connections within New York's political, business, and social circles were vast. He was known to attend lavish fundraisers, often rubbing shoulders with influential figures from across the state and beyond. Many saw these events as a necessary part of political life, especially in a city as large and complex as New York. But federal prosecutors began to wonder whether these gatherings were more than just social occasions. Were they, in fact, fronts for something far more nefarious?

The investigation gained momentum when a whistleblower from within Adams's campaign came forward, alleging that the mayor and his team had been accepting illegal campaign donations. These weren't just any donations—they were coming from foreign entities, a clear violation of U.S. law. The whistleblower's claims were explosive, but at the time, they lacked the evidence needed to proceed. Still, it was enough to spark a deeper look into Adams's fundraising efforts. Investigators began combing through years of campaign finance records, tracking donations and looking for inconsistencies.

It was during this period that federal prosecutors discovered a series of wire transfers that seemed to be connected to foreign donors. These funds, which had been funneled through a complex web of intermediaries, eventually found their way into Adams's campaign coffers. The sums were significant, but even more concerning was the nature of the donors themselves. Some had direct ties to foreign governments, while others appeared to be part of international business syndicates with interests in New York real estate. For investigators, this raised a red flag. What could these foreign entities possibly hope to gain by supporting the mayor of New York City?

As the investigation deepened, more witnesses were brought in for questioning. Some were members of Adams's inner circle, people who had worked closely with him on his campaign. Others were political operatives, donors, and business leaders who had attended his fundraisers. Slowly but surely, a picture began to emerge. It wasn't just that Adams had accepted illegal donations—there were also allegations of bribery. According to some witnesses, donors who had contributed large sums to Adams's campaign were later rewarded with lucrative city contracts or favourable policy decisions.

The idea that a sitting mayor could be involved in such activities sent shockwaves through the political establishment. For years, Adams had been seen as a reformer, someone who understood the challenges of governing a city as diverse and complicated as New York. Now, he was at the centre of a federal investigation that threatened not just his political career, but the integrity of the entire city government.

The media caught wind of the investigation long before any formal charges were filed. At first, the coverage was limited to whispers and speculation. Rumours swirled that Adams was being investigated, but there was little concrete evidence to support these claims. Still, the mere suggestion that the mayor could be under federal scrutiny was enough to cause concern among his allies. Many of them began distancing themselves from Adams, quietly preparing for the possibility that his administration could be engulfed in scandal.

As the investigation continued, Adams maintained his innocence. Publicly, he downplayed the rumours, insisting that his campaign had always followed the rules. He pointed to his long track record of public service, reminding New Yorkers that he had spent decades fighting for the people of the city. Privately, however, Adams was reportedly growing increasingly anxious. He knew that the investigation had the potential to derail not just his mayoralty, but everything he had worked for over the course of his career.

Behind closed doors, Adams's legal team began preparing for the worst. They knew that federal investigators were building a case, and they knew that it was only a matter of time before charges were filed. Still, they remained hopeful that the case could be settled quietly, without the need for a public trial. But as the months went on, it became clear that the federal government was not going to let this case slip away.

In the spring of 2024, federal prosecutors made their move. The indictment was unsealed, revealing a litany of charges against Adams, including wire fraud, bribery, and accepting illegal campaign donations. The charges were serious, and they carried the potential for significant prison time if Adams were found guilty. The news sent shockwaves through the city, as New Yorkers grappled with the possibility that their mayor could soon be facing trial.

The reaction from the political establishment was swift. Many of Adams's former allies, who had once praised his leadership, now called for his resignation. Even those who had supported him throughout his career began to distance themselves, unwilling to be associated with the growing scandal. For Adams, the fallout was devastating. His once-promising political career was now in jeopardy, and his legacy as mayor was at risk of being defined by the charges against him.

The federal investigation into Adams was a slow burn, one that took years to come to fruition. But when it finally did, it came with the full force of the U.S. legal system. The charges against him were the culmination of years of scrutiny, a reminder that in politics, even the most powerful figures are not above the law. As Adams prepared to face his day in court, the people of New York were left to wonder what would come next. Would their mayor be vindicated, or would he become the latest in a long line of New York politicians brought down by scandal?

The investigation into Adams was not just about one man—it was a reflection of the larger issues facing New York City's political system. For years, questions had been raised about the influence of money in politics, the role of donors, and the ways in which power is wielded in one of the largest and most complex cities in the world. The investigation into Adams brought these issues to the forefront, forcing New Yorkers to confront the reality that their city's political system was not as clean as they might have hoped. And as the trial loomed on the horizon, one thing was clear: the story of Eric Adams was far from over.

Chapter 5: The Indictment

The Charges: Wire Fraud, Bribery, and Campaign Violations

The indictment of New York City Mayor Eric Adams marked a pivotal moment not just in his political career but in the city's governance. For a man who had risen from a modest background, worked his way through the ranks of the NYPD, and eventually secured the highest office in one of the most powerful cities in the world, the charges against him felt like a seismic shift. The allegations included wire fraud, bribery, and campaign violations—serious accusations that threatened not only his future but the stability of New York's political landscape.

Adams, who had long positioned himself as a champion of law and order, found himself under federal scrutiny. This irony was not lost on the public, nor on the legal minds involved in his prosecution. The charges stemmed from a complex, years-long investigation that delved into his actions as both Brooklyn borough president and mayor, suggesting that the behaviour in question had roots going back several years. The indictment itself, unsealed after intense speculation, revealed a tangled web of allegations centered on financial misconduct, unethical relationships, and questionable campaign practices.

At the heart of the indictment were accusations of wire fraud. Wire fraud, a federal crime involving the use of telecommunications or information technology to defraud, can encompass a wide variety of actions. In Adams's case, prosecutors alleged that he had engaged in deceptive practices to solicit and accept illegal campaign donations. These donations were not only illegal in their origin—coming from foreign sources prohibited from influencing American elections—but were also funneled through intermediaries and shell companies to disguise their true nature. This web of deceit was meticulously planned, according to federal prosecutors, making it appear that Adams's campaign was above board when, in reality, it was steeped in unethical conduct.

One of the most damning aspects of the indictment was the involvement of foreign actors. The allegations suggested that Adams had knowingly accepted donations from individuals and entities based abroad, a violation of U.S. law. Foreign involvement in American elections is strictly regulated, with good reason. The idea that foreign powers or interests could influence local or national elections runs counter to the foundational principles of democracy. In Adams's case, the indictment painted a picture of a candidate who was not just oblivious to these rules, but actively engaged in subverting them for personal and political gain.

The bribery charges were equally damaging, casting a shadow over Adams's reputation. Bribery, particularly in political circles, is viewed as one of the most egregious forms of corruption. The charge against Adams suggested that he had accepted money and favours in exchange for political influence, using his position to reward those who financially backed him. The investigation uncovered evidence that Adams had engaged in quid-pro-quo relationships, where donors were rewarded with special access, political favours, and contracts that benefitted their businesses. These actions, according to the indictment, were part of a broader pattern of corruption that undermined the trust that the public had placed in him.

One particularly disturbing element of the bribery charges was how closely it tied to his work as Brooklyn borough president. During his tenure in this role, Adams had significant control over various contracts and permits. Prosecutors argued that he had used this influence to benefit those who had supported his rise to power. This behaviour, which spanned several years, followed him into his role as mayor, where he was accused of continuing these unethical practices on a grander scale.

The campaign violations outlined in the indictment were multifaceted and ranged from misreporting donations to using improper financial channels to fund his campaigns. These actions were not just technical violations but indicative of a broader disregard for the legal framework designed to ensure fair and transparent elections. Adams's campaign, prosecutors argued, had intentionally obscured the source of its funds, making it nearly impossible for election officials and the public to understand where his financial backing came from. This lack of transparency, they said, eroded public trust and raised serious questions about his ability to lead the city with integrity.

Beyond the legal specifics, the indictment was also a story of power, ambition, and the darker side of political life. Adams, once a symbol of hope for many in New York, was now caught up in a scandal that could define his career. The charges cast doubt not only on his personal ethics but also on the broader political machine that had helped him rise to power. For years, critics had accused New York's political landscape of being rife with corruption, and Adams's indictment seemed to confirm many of those suspicions.

For many New Yorkers, the indictment was a sobering reminder of the challenges that come with political power. The mayor's office, a symbol of leadership and accountability, was now embroiled in a scandal that called into question the very principles it was meant to uphold. The wire fraud, bribery, and campaign violations laid out in the indictment suggested a pattern of behaviour that went beyond mere oversight or poor judgment. Instead, they painted a picture of a politician who was willing to bend or break the rules to further his own career.

Adams, for his part, was defiant in the face of these allegations. At press conferences, he maintained his innocence, insisting that he had followed the law and that the charges against him were politically motivated. He urged the public to wait for the full story to emerge, confident that his legal team would dismantle the prosecution's case. His supporters echoed these sentiments, arguing that the charges were overblown and that Adams was being targeted unfairly because of his position.

Yet, despite his protests, the weight of the indictment was undeniable. The charges brought against him threatened not only his career but also the future of his political allies and the city itself. As the legal process unfolded, questions arose about whether Adams could effectively govern while facing such serious accusations. Could he continue to lead the city with the integrity and focus required, or would the cloud of scandal overshadow every decision he made?

The indictment also had far-reaching implications for New York's political future. With elections looming, many wondered how the scandal would impact voter turnout, party loyalty, and the overall perception of leadership in the city. For Adams's opponents, the indictment provided ammunition to question his credibility and suitability for office. For his supporters, it was a test of loyalty and patience, as they waited to see how the legal process would play out.

In the end, the indictment of Eric Adams was more than just a legal matter—it was a defining moment for the city he led. The charges of wire fraud, bribery, and campaign violations raised serious questions about the integrity of New York's political system and the future of its leadership. As the case moved through the courts, the city waited, unsure of what would come next but keenly aware that the outcome would have lasting repercussions.

The legal battle ahead promised to be long and complicated, with both sides preparing for a protracted fight. For Adams, the stakes were clear: his reputation, his career, and the legacy he had worked so hard to build hung in the balance. For the people of New York, the indictment was a reminder of the fragile nature of power and the importance of holding leaders accountable. Whatever the outcome, the charges against Adams would leave an indelible mark on the city's political landscape, shaping its future in ways that few could predict.

Chapter 6: The Public and Political Response

Reactions from New York Democrats and National Figures

The indictment of New York City Mayor Eric Adams on bribery charges sent shockwaves through the city and the national political landscape. In a city where political scandals have occasionally surfaced, Adams' fall from grace was particularly jarring. A mayor who had come into office promising to restore order, reduce crime, and bring efficiency to City Hall, Adams now found himself at the centre of a legal storm. As the news of the federal charges broke, the responses from political allies, opponents, and everyday New Yorkers revealed much about the current state of politics, not only in New York but across the nation.

Among his colleagues in the Democratic Party, the reaction was largely one of shock and disappointment. Many New York Democrats had pinned their hopes on Adams as a figure who could unite the city and address its pressing challenges. He had presented himself as a leader capable of balancing progressivism with pragmatism, appealing to both left-leaning voters and more moderate constituents. But now, with allegations of wire fraud, bribery, and illegal campaign donations, his reputation was on the line. Despite the gravity of the charges, most Democrats initially stopped short of demanding his resignation, preferring instead to let the legal process unfold.

House Minority Leader Hakeem Jeffries, a prominent New York Democrat, expressed a cautious response that echoed through many political circles. Jeffries, who had often praised Adams' leadership, released a carefully worded statement highlighting the principle of the presumption of innocence. His remarks focused on the notion that in America, even public officials are entitled to a fair trial. Jeffries' approach was reflective of a broader strategy among New York Democrats to navigate the crisis without prematurely distancing themselves from the embattled mayor. For many, the priority was to ensure that the charges did not overshadow the broader Democratic agenda in the city and the state.

The delicate balance between supporting Adams and maintaining political integrity was evident in the response of Senate Majority Leader Chuck Schumer. As the highest-ranking Democrat from New York, Schumer's statement underscored the seriousness of the charges while urging that the legal process be allowed to play out swiftly and fairly. Schumer's response was notable for its careful phrasing. He neither condemned Adams outright nor offered a full-throated defense. Instead, like many other Democrats, Schumer chose to maintain a measured tone, reflecting the understanding that any overt attack on Adams could have unpredictable political consequences.

However, not all Democrats were content to wait for the legal system to decide Adams' fate. Congresswoman Alexandria Ocasio-Cortez (AOC), a high-profile progressive figure, was one of the first to call for Adams' resignation. Even before the formal indictment was announced, AOC had publicly criticised the ongoing investigations surrounding the mayor, arguing that they had already eroded public trust in his ability to govern effectively. In her view, the constant cloud of suspicion hanging over Adams made it impossible for him to lead New York City with the authority and credibility required of a mayor. AOC's call for Adams' resignation was rooted in her broader critique of political corruption and her vision of a more transparent, accountable government.

For some Democrats, the legal charges against Adams represented not only a personal failing but also a broader challenge to the party's credibility. Figures like Congresswoman Nydia Velázquez, while not explicitly demanding Adams' resignation, strongly suggested that his ability to govern had been irreparably compromised. In an interview, Velázquez noted that if she were in Adams' position, she would step down, acknowledging the difficulty of leading a city like New York while under such intense scrutiny. Her comments reflected a growing sentiment within certain segments of the Democratic Party that the scandal, regardless of its eventual outcome, had already tainted Adams' administration beyond repair.

The political ramifications of Adams' indictment extended beyond New York City, particularly as Republicans seized on the scandal to attack Democrats in key congressional races. With several contested seats on Long Island and in the Hudson Valley, Republicans were quick to tie Adams' legal troubles to broader critiques of Democratic leadership in New York. The GOP strategy was clear: use Adams' downfall as a symbol of what they portrayed as Democratic corruption and incompetence. This approach echoed tactics used in previous election cycles, where Republicans had successfully capitalised on issues like crime and immigration to gain traction in suburban districts.

Republican leaders wasted no time in framing the Adams indictment as part of a larger narrative about the failings of Democratic governance. Congresswoman Elise Stefanik, chair of the House GOP conference, issued a blistering statement calling for Adams' resignation and accusing the Democratic Party of being rife with corruption. Stefanik's remarks drew a direct line between Adams' legal troubles and those of former Governor Andrew Cuomo, who had resigned amid sexual harassment allegations in 2021. For Republicans, Adams' indictment was not just an isolated scandal but a reflection of a broader culture of corruption within the New York Democratic establishment.

Despite the harsh rhetoric from Republicans, many Democrats remained focused on maintaining a unified front. Political strategists within the party were acutely aware of the potential fallout from Adams' indictment, especially in tight races. While some candidates, particularly those in swing districts, sought to distance themselves from the mayor, others took a more cautious approach, emphasising the importance of due process and the presumption of innocence. The overarching goal for many Democrats was to prevent the Adams scandal from becoming a defining issue in the upcoming elections.

The public response to Adams' indictment was similarly varied. Among everyday New Yorkers, opinions ranged from outrage to ambivalence. Some saw the charges as yet another example of corruption in a city that has seen its fair share of political scandals. Others expressed disappointment, having believed in Adams' promise to bring change and stability to New York. In neighbourhoods where Adams had built strong support, particularly in Brooklyn, there was a sense of betrayal among some voters who had hoped he would lead the city through its most pressing challenges, including crime, homelessness, and economic recovery.

At the same time, there were those who remained supportive of Adams, viewing the charges as politically motivated or overblown. In interviews with local media, some of Adams' constituents voiced their belief that the mayor was being unfairly targeted, pointing to his efforts to address public safety and reform city governance. For these supporters, Adams represented a break from the status quo, and they were willing to give him the benefit of the doubt as the legal process unfolded.

Nationally, the Adams scandal garnered attention as part of a broader conversation about political corruption and accountability. In an era where public trust in government institutions is already fragile, the indictment of a major city's mayor raised questions about the ethical standards of elected officials. Political commentators weighed in on the implications of the charges, with some suggesting that the Adams case could serve as a cautionary tale for politicians across the country. Others noted that the scandal was emblematic of the challenges faced by urban leaders who must navigate complex political and financial networks while striving to maintain public trust.

As the legal proceedings against Adams moved forward, the public and political responses continued to evolve. For many, the case served as a reminder of the fragility of political power and the importance of accountability. While Adams had come into office with high hopes and a bold vision for New York City, his indictment marked a turning point not only for his administration but for the city's political landscape. Whether he would ultimately be convicted or acquitted, the scandal had already left an indelible mark on his legacy and the future of New York politics.

In the weeks and months following the indictment, the city's political class continued to grapple with the fallout. Some leaders doubled down on their calls for reform, emphasising the need for greater transparency and oversight in campaign financing and political governance. Others remained focused on the immediate task of navigating the legal complexities of the case. For New Yorkers, the indictment of their mayor was a sobering reminder of the challenges inherent in balancing ambition, power, and integrity in public life.

Chapter 7: The Legal Battle

Adams's Defence and the Legal Proceedings

The legal battle that ensued following the indictment of Eric Adams was nothing short of dramatic. It brought with it not just the weight of federal accusations but the glare of public scrutiny on a man who, only months before, had been seen as a promising leader with ambitions to reshape New York City. For Adams, the fight to clear his name was more than a battle in the courtroom; it was a fight for his political survival and reputation.

From the moment the charges were made public, Adams faced a dual challenge: convincing the legal system of his innocence and maintaining the trust of the city's residents. His defence team, composed of some of the most renowned legal minds in the country, quickly went to work. Their primary task was to dismantle the complex web of charges levied against the mayor—charges that ranged from wire fraud to bribery, all rooted in allegations of accepting illegal campaign donations from foreign entities.

Eric Adams's public persona, which had always revolved around transparency and the desire to make the city safer and more inclusive, became a significant part of his defence strategy. His legal team wasted no time in painting the picture of a man who had dedicated his life to serving the people, from his early years in the New York Police Department to his time as Brooklyn borough president. This narrative of a committed public servant became the bedrock of the argument that Adams was the victim of an overzealous investigation, rather than a willing participant in any criminal activity.

In the courtroom, Adams's defence team sought to challenge the prosecution's evidence at every turn. One of the most critical aspects of the case was the alleged illegal campaign donations. Federal prosecutors had traced funds from foreign sources into Adams's campaign, suggesting that these funds had been funneled to him in exchange for political favors. The defence countered this narrative by asserting that Adams had no direct knowledge of the origin of the donations and had relied on his campaign staff to ensure compliance with legal guidelines. They pointed out that, as a mayoral candidate, Adams was engaged in the whirlwind of the campaign trail, often removed from the finer details of campaign financing.

Furthermore, the defence questioned the credibility of key witnesses brought forward by the prosecution. Some of these individuals had close ties to Adams's political rivals or had their own reasons for cooperating with the authorities. Adams's lawyers worked tirelessly to cast doubt on their testimonies, suggesting that their motivations were tainted by self-interest rather than a genuine desire for justice. This line of defence sought to weaken the foundation of the prosecution's case, raising the possibility that Adams was being targeted for reasons beyond mere legal culpability.

Throughout the proceedings, Adams maintained his innocence, often making public statements where he expressed his faith in the justice system and his determination to clear his name. In one of his more memorable speeches outside the courtroom, Adams stood resolute, surrounded by supporters, as he declared, "I have spent my entire career upholding the law, and I would never compromise the trust of the people of New York." These public displays of confidence, while carefully crafted, were intended to reassure New Yorkers that their mayor was still capable of leading the city despite the mounting legal troubles.

Behind closed doors, however, the atmosphere was tense. The prosecution had meticulously built its case over several years, and they had access to a trove of financial records, communication logs, and testimony that they believed would prove Adams's involvement in illegal activities. The sheer volume of evidence presented posed a significant hurdle for Adams's defence team, forcing them to scrutinise every document and every interaction the mayor had had during his campaign and early time in office.

One of the key turning points in the trial came when the defence introduced evidence suggesting that Adams had, in fact, taken steps to ensure his campaign followed legal donation guidelines. Internal emails and memos were brought forward showing that Adams had directed his staff to be thorough in their vetting processes for donations. His legal team argued that while mistakes might have been made, they were not due to intentional misconduct on Adams's part, but rather a byproduct of the chaotic nature of political campaigns.

This line of argument resonated with some observers. Political campaigns, especially those at the mayoral level in a city as large as New York, are often frenetic, fast-paced affairs where candidates rely heavily on their staff to manage the intricacies of campaign law. Adams's defence contended that he had delegated responsibility to individuals he trusted, and while they may have erred, it did not mean that Adams himself was complicit in any wrongdoing.

Still, the prosecution pushed back hard, emphasising that as the head of the campaign, Adams had a duty to ensure all aspects of his operation were above board. They argued that even if Adams had not directly orchestrated the illegal donations, he had created an environment where such behaviour was possible by failing to enforce stricter oversight. This argument was crucial in shaping the perception of Adams as either a negligent leader or a man caught in an unfortunate series of events.

As the trial progressed, it became clear that public opinion was deeply divided. Some saw Adams as the unfortunate victim of a politically motivated investigation, while others believed the charges were an indictment of the larger corruption that had plagued New York politics for years. The media played a significant role in shaping these narratives, with news outlets often framing the trial as either a witch hunt or a long-overdue reckoning.

Throughout it all, Adams remained a central figure in the courtroom. His calm demeanour and consistent declarations of innocence stood in stark contrast to the gravity of the charges against him. He appeared regularly at press conferences, addressing the city's ongoing issues and asserting his capability to lead despite the legal proceedings. This was a deliberate move by his legal team, who knew that, in the court of public opinion, showing strength under pressure could be just as important as the outcome of the trial itself.

In the final stages of the trial, both sides made impassioned arguments. The prosecution urged the jury to consider the broader implications of Adams's actions, framing the case as one about the integrity of public office. The defence, meanwhile, appealed to the jury's sense of fairness, insisting that Adams had not deliberately broken the law and that convicting him would be an unjust outcome for a man who had dedicated his life to serving the city.

As the jury deliberated, the tension in New York City was palpable. The outcome of the trial would have far-reaching consequences, not just for Adams but for the future of the city's political landscape. Regardless of the verdict, one thing was certain: the legal battle had fundamentally changed the trajectory of Eric Adams's career. He had gone from a rising star in New York politics to a figure embroiled in scandal, fighting for his reputation and his political future.

In the end, the legal proceedings surrounding Eric Adams would be remembered not just for the courtroom drama but for the larger questions they raised about accountability, leadership, and the intersection of law and politics. For Adams, the battle may have been about proving his innocence, but for the people of New York, it was about whether they could continue to trust the leaders they had elected to serve them.

Chapter 8: Impact on New York Politics

The Fallout: How the Scandal Shook New York's Political Landscape

The indictment of Mayor Eric Adams on charges of bribery and wire fraud sent shockwaves through New York's political establishment. For a city as politically charged and influential as New York, the impact of such a high-profile scandal on both local and state politics was immediate and far-reaching. The accusations against Adams, coming at a time of significant economic and social challenges for the city, exacerbated existing tensions within New York's political fabric and raised questions about the future leadership of one of the world's most important cities.

From the moment the charges were made public, the reactions among political allies and rivals were swift. Eric Adams, who had built his reputation as a tough, reform-minded leader, now found himself embroiled in a scandal that could not only end his political career but also tarnish the broader Democratic Party in New York. The state's political leadership, already navigating a landscape marked by battles over issues like crime, housing, and migration, had to contend with the fallout from Adams's indictment, as it threatened to undermine the trust voters had in the party's ability to govern effectively.

One of the most significant impacts of the scandal was its timing. With the indictment landing just a month before a critical election cycle, Democrats across the state found themselves on the defensive. Many were scrambling to distance themselves from Adams while trying to maintain unity within a party that was already under pressure. The Republicans, sensing an opportunity, capitalized on the situation to strengthen their campaigns, particularly in swing districts where the mayor's legal troubles became a focal point. The scandal gave the GOP an opening to attack not just Adams but the entire Democratic establishment in New York, framing it as riddled with corruption and mismanagement.

For years, Republicans had used issues like crime and migration in New York City to rally their base, particularly in suburban areas such as Long Island and the Hudson Valley. With Adams now facing charges, these attacks gained new potency.

Republican candidates in key House races seized on the scandal, drawing parallels between Adams and other controversial figures in New York politics, such as former Governor Andrew Cuomo. The message was clear: corruption was rampant among New York's Democratic leaders, and it was time for a change. This narrative resonated in key battleground districts, where voters were already frustrated with rising crime rates and concerns over the city's handling of economic recovery.

At the state level, Governor Kathy Hochul also felt the ripple effects of the scandal. Hochul, who had supported Adams during his campaign for mayor and had worked closely with him on several key initiatives, now faced criticism for her association with him. Although she was not directly implicated in the scandal, the perception of political ties between the two became a talking point for her opponents. Some political commentators argued that her administration's credibility had taken a hit, and that she would need to work hard to restore public confidence in her leadership. Her critics began to question her judgment in aligning with a figure now accused of corruption, further complicating her own political future.

The scandal also had a polarizing effect within the Democratic Party itself. While many leading figures, such as House Minority Leader Hakeem Jeffries and Senate Majority Leader Chuck Schumer, took a measured approach, calling for the legal process to run its course and maintaining that Adams was entitled to the presumption of innocence, others were less forgiving. Progressive voices within the party, led by figures like Rep. Alexandria Ocasio-Cortez, were more vocal in their calls for Adams to step down, arguing that the investigations surrounding him had already eroded the public's trust in his leadership. Ocasio-Cortez's call for his resignation highlighted the growing divide within the party, where establishment Democrats and the progressive wing were increasingly at odds over the direction of the party and its leadership.

For New York City, the scandal created a leadership vacuum at a critical time. Adams had been elected on a platform of reform and revitalization, promising to tackle some of the city's most pressing issues, including crime, economic inequality, and housing. With these challenges still at the forefront, the indictment threatened to derail progress on these key issues, as the mayor's focus inevitably shifted to defending himself in court. This shift left many New Yorkers wondering who would step up to address the city's problems in the midst of such political turmoil.

The scandal also posed serious questions about the integrity of the city's political system. New York City has long been known for its rough-and-tumble politics, with corruption scandals emerging periodically over the years. However, the allegations against Adams seemed particularly damaging because they hit at the heart of his campaign message: that he was a reformer who would clean up city government. The charges of accepting illegal campaign donations from foreign sources were especially troubling, as they suggested not just ethical lapses, but violations of federal law.

In the immediate aftermath of the indictment, there were calls for reforms to campaign finance laws and more robust oversight of city officials. Some argued that Adams's downfall could be a catalyst for meaningful change, forcing the city to confront its long-standing issues with political corruption. However, others were more cynical, suggesting that the scandal was simply the latest chapter in a long history of corruption in New York politics, and that real reform would be difficult to achieve.

As the legal process unfolded, the uncertainty surrounding Adams's future also cast a shadow over the city's upcoming policy initiatives. With the mayor's credibility in question, it became harder for his administration to push forward with its legislative agenda. Key policy proposals, such as plans to address the city's homelessness crisis and revitalize the economy, were met with increased skepticism. Many city officials and legislators were reluctant to align themselves too closely with an embattled mayor, fearing that their own political futures could be jeopardized by association.

The ripple effects of the scandal were felt far beyond New York City. Nationally, the indictment of such a high-profile Democratic figure provided fodder for Republicans seeking to gain ground in the 2024 elections. It also reinforced a narrative that had been gaining traction in conservative circles: that Democratic-run cities were plagued by crime, corruption, and ineffective governance. For Republicans, the Adams scandal was a gift, allowing them to draw attention to the perceived failures of

Democratic leadership in New York while bolstering their own candidates in key congressional races.

In the end, the indictment of Eric Adams had a profound impact on New York politics. It not only disrupted the mayor's administration but also reshaped the political landscape across the state. The scandal amplified divisions within the Democratic Party, weakened the party's position in key electoral districts, and raised serious questions about the future leadership of New York City.

Whether or not Adams is ultimately convicted, the fallout from the scandal will likely be felt for years to come, as New Yorkers grapple with the broader implications of having a mayor who faces serious legal challenges. For now, the city remains in a state of political limbo, waiting to see whether it can recover from the shockwaves of a scandal that has shaken its political core.

Chapter 9: Eric Adams's Legacy

From Promising Leader to Embattled Mayor: What's Left of His Career

Eric Adams's rise to power was marked by ambition, resilience, and a genuine passion for public service. From his early days in the NYPD to becoming Brooklyn's borough president, Adams carved out a reputation as a reformer, an advocate for the underrepresented, and someone deeply committed to the city he served. His journey to becoming mayor was one that many saw as the pinnacle of a long and dedicated career in public service. Yet, the very qualities that once made him a beacon of hope for many in New York City have now been overshadowed by the legal controversies and the bribery scandal that has engulfed his time in office.

Adams's early days as mayor were filled with high expectations. He came into office with the promise of reforming a city that had been battered by the COVID-19 pandemic, with increasing concerns about public safety, economic recovery, and housing instability. His experience as a police officer gave him unique insights into the challenges New York City faced in terms of crime and law enforcement, and many voters believed he was the right person to balance the delicate relationship between police reform and public safety. His platform resonated with a broad spectrum of voters, from working-class families to business leaders, all of whom were eager for stability and leadership after a tumultuous period.

However, as his administration progressed, cracks began to show. His commitment to overhauling the city's approach to public safety was met with resistance from various sides. Critics argued that Adams's close ties to law enforcement made him less capable of pushing for necessary reforms, while others contended that his focus on crime prevention detracted from addressing the broader socioeconomic issues that plagued the city. Nonetheless, Adams pressed on, confident in his ability to navigate the political landscape and deliver on his promises. His tenacity and confidence, which had once been seen as strengths, soon became a double-edged sword.

The federal indictment that would come to define the latter part of Adams's career was a blow not only to his administration but to the city itself. Accusations of bribery, wire fraud, and accepting illegal campaign donations from abroad were shocking, not just because of the nature of the charges but because of who Adams had been perceived to be. For someone who had built his career on integrity, fairness, and advocacy for the underserved, the charges seemed to contradict everything he stood for. The indictment was the culmination of a long investigation that began during his time as Brooklyn borough president, making it clear that these issues had been brewing long before his time as mayor.

As the scandal unfolded, the city's political environment grew increasingly tense. Adams's supporters, who had once lauded him for his leadership, were now forced to reckon with the possibility that their mayor had engaged in illegal activities. Many of his allies distanced themselves, urging the public to wait for the legal process to play out. Yet, the damage was done. Adams's administration, which had already been grappling with internal challenges, now had to contend with the public relations nightmare that comes with federal charges. The perception of Adams as a leader was fundamentally altered.

What remains most heartbreaking about Adams's fall from grace is how much potential there was for his administration to enact meaningful change. He had the experience, the knowledge, and the passion to guide the city through a difficult period, but the scandal has overshadowed these qualities. His legacy, now tainted by allegations of corruption, has become a cautionary tale about the dangers of political ambition unchecked by transparency and accountability. For a city like New York, where trust in government officials is already precarious, the scandal dealt a significant blow to public confidence.

Despite the ongoing legal battles, Adams's defiance has remained steadfast. In public statements, he has maintained his innocence, insisting that he has always followed the law and campaign regulations. His refusal to step down, even amid calls from some within his own party, highlights the complex nature of political survival in an era where scandals are met with both outrage and cynicism. For Adams, the decision to remain in office while fighting these charges could be seen as a testament to his resilience or as a refusal to acknowledge the gravity of the situation. Either way, his choice has only intensified the public's scrutiny of his leadership.

One of the most significant impacts of this scandal is its effect on Adams's broader political ambitions. There was a time when many believed that his tenure as mayor could serve as a stepping stone to higher office, perhaps even a national platform. His appeal as a former police officer-turned-politician who could navigate both sides of the political spectrum made him a formidable figure in New York politics. However, the indictment has all but dashed these prospects. Even if he is acquitted or if the charges are dropped, the damage to his reputation is likely irreversible. The trust that voters once placed in him has been deeply eroded, and it will take more than a legal victory to restore his credibility.

Beyond Adams's personal legacy, this scandal has also raised broader questions about corruption in New York politics. The city has seen its fair share of political scandals, from former Governor Andrew Cuomo's resignation to various local officials being implicated in wrongdoing. Adams's case adds to the narrative that New York's political system is rife with corruption, further disillusioning an already skeptical public. The implications for future political leaders are significant. In an era where transparency and accountability are increasingly demanded, any hint of impropriety can have long-lasting effects on a politician's career.

As Adams's legal battles continue, the city is left to grapple with the uncertainty of its future leadership. While he remains in office for the time being, many question whether he can effectively govern while dealing with such serious allegations. The pressure from his constituents, political allies, and opponents continues to mount. His administration's ability to enact meaningful policies has been stymied by the scandal, leaving many of the city's most pressing issues unresolved.

Adams's legacy will be defined not just by the charges brought against him but by how he responds to this moment of crisis. Will he be remembered as a promising leader who fell victim to his own ambition, or will he find a way to salvage his career and restore some semblance of the hope that once surrounded his name? The answer remains uncertain, but one thing is clear: the trajectory of his career, once filled with promise, has taken a dramatic and perhaps irreversible turn.

The story of Eric Adams is a reminder that political success is fragile, and the qualities that elevate someone to power can also be their undoing. For Adams, his legacy is no longer just about his accomplishments but about the scandal that has come to define his time in office. Whether he can rise above it or whether it will mark the end of his political journey remains to be seen, but the consequences of his actions will undoubtedly shape the future of New York City for years to come.

What's Next for Eric Adams and New York City?

As the legal proceedings unfold, Eric Adams finds himself at a crossroads, one that could not only determine his political future but also shape the trajectory of New York City's leadership for years to come. The charges brought against Adams—wire fraud, bribery, and accepting illegal campaign donations—are serious, casting a long shadow over the mayor's administration and threatening to derail what was once a promising political career. Yet, amidst the allegations and the mounting public scrutiny, one key question looms large: what's next for both Eric Adams and the city he governs?

For Adams, the future appears uncertain, and his response to the indictment will play a crucial role in determining whether he can salvage any of his political credibility. Defiant in the face of the charges, Adams has consistently denied any wrongdoing, maintaining that he has always followed the law and asking the public to reserve judgment until his defense is fully heard. However, even as he seeks to clear his name, the sheer weight of the allegations against him, combined with the public nature of his role as mayor, makes it difficult for him to govern effectively.

One of the major obstacles Adams faces is the erosion of public trust. A mayor's ability to lead rests heavily on the faith and confidence of the people he serves, and once that trust is compromised, regaining it becomes a near-impossible task. Even if Adams were to be exonerated in court, the cloud of scandal may linger in the public consciousness, forever altering his image and reputation. The constant investigations and media attention surrounding his case have already raised questions about his ability to perform the duties of his office without distraction, with critics arguing that the scandal has undermined his capacity to govern the largest city in the United States.

As Adams navigates this difficult period, the city of New York also finds itself in a precarious position. The indictment has come at a time when the city is grappling with a multitude of challenges, from economic recovery in the wake of the COVID-19 pandemic to rising concerns about public safety and housing shortages. Adams, who campaigned on promises to address many of these issues, now faces the reality that his ability to implement meaningful change may be severely hindered by his legal troubles. Without a strong and stable leadership, the city risks falling further into political disarray, as confidence in the mayor's office diminishes.

The potential outcomes for Adams are stark. If convicted, his tenure as mayor would almost certainly come to an abrupt end, likely through resignation or removal from office. This would trigger a new political battle over who would succeed him, throwing New York City's already volatile political landscape into further chaos. The public advocate, who would assume the role of acting mayor, may not have the political clout or the public support to steer the city through such turbulent times. This would leave New York at a critical juncture, with the possibility of prolonged political instability as new elections loom.

On the other hand, if Adams is acquitted or the charges are somehow dismissed, he could attempt to reclaim his role as a functioning leader of the city. However, even an acquittal would not erase the damage that has already been done. The scandals and accusations will likely remain a stain on his political career, providing fodder for opponents and casting doubt on his integrity. Rebuilding the trust of New Yorkers would be an uphill battle, and many may question whether Adams can truly recover from such a public fall from grace.

For the city itself, the long-term effects of Adams's legal woes are hard to predict, but they are likely to have ripple effects across various sectors. Politically, the scandal has already been seized upon by Republicans, both locally and nationally, as a way to critique the Democratic Party's leadership in New York. With key congressional seats in play, particularly in suburban areas like Long Island, the indictment of a high-profile Democratic mayor could serve as a talking point for Republicans eager to win votes in traditionally blue districts. If Adams's troubles continue to dominate headlines, the scandal could also impact future mayoral elections, as candidates distance themselves from the tainted administration and look to present themselves as ethical and transparent alternatives.

Economically, New York City needs strong leadership to continue its post-pandemic recovery, attract new businesses, and retain its status as a global hub for commerce and tourism. The uncertainty surrounding the mayor's office could deter investment and weaken the city's ability to navigate the complex issues it currently faces. Residents, too, may feel the strain of leadership in limbo, as public services and critical city projects suffer from lack of direction or clear decision-making at the top.

The story of Eric Adams is far from over. Whether he survives this scandal or succumbs to its pressures will depend on the legal system's outcome and the political maneuvering that follows. Regardless of what happens, the implications for New York City are profound. The city stands at a pivotal moment, and how it emerges from this crisis—whether with new leadership or a weakened administration—will shape its future for years to come. Adams's next steps, and the decisions of those around him, will determine whether this chapter in New York's history is one of recovery or further decline.